© Jennifer Jackson, CCLC, CPBF
Rhythms of the Soul, 2020

ALL TRADEMARKS ARE ACKNOWLEDGED.

Cover photo credit: Danny Herrera

Every effort has been made to ensure that the information contained in this document is true and correct at the time of going to press.

However, the networks, systems, products, processes, specifications, and content in general described in this document are subject to continuous development and author is entitled to change them at any time and to expand on them.

Jennifer Jackson nor Rhythms of the Soul cannot accept liability for any loss or damage of any nature whatsoever arising or resulting from the use of or reliance on information or particulars in this document.

All names and other data used in examples are fictitious. The information contained in this document is of a general nature. Should you require further advice for your particular business requirements, please refer to the contact details below.

No part of this document may be reproduced by any means, other than with the express written permission of the Author.

TO CONTACT PLEASE WRITE OR EMAIL:

Jennifer Jackson, CCLC, CPBF
Rhythms of the Soul
2900 Adams Street, C-255
Riverside, CA 92504

Email:
jenni@rhythmsofthesoul.com

Contents

INTRODUCTION .... P. 1

THE CALM BEFORE THE STORM .... P. 4

THE WAVES ARE RISING .... P. 19

THE PLAN .... P. 29

THE CYCLE .... P. 40

RETHINK .... P. 52

REVIEW .... P. 64

ASSERTIVENESS & CONFLICT RESOLUTION .... P. 72

HEREDITY OR HABIT .... P. 84

FINAL REVIEW .... P. 99

CLOSING THOUGHTS .... P. 109

GROUP FACILITATOR GUIDE .... P. 110

Introduction....

Have you ever been in a situation or conversation and before you realize it you are feeling the storm of anger, or rage? You can feel this energy surging through your body. You may feel tension all over or possibly just in specific areas of your body. Then without even thinking you say or do things that are so far from who you are or what you wanted to express.

Your emotions do not seem to match with the situation you are in or what you are even discussing. This can be a huge struggle for some of us. I know it was for me.

Relationships can be damaged beyond repair and it happens in an instant. We can be calm one second, engaging with a person and before we realize it we are yelling and saying mean and hurtful things.

Painful things to a person we love or someone we care about. Worse yet, we can act out physically and cause damage to things, or even worse yet hurt someone physically and have severe traumatic consequences for all involved.

Afterwards we may find ourselves filled with shame and we don't have to tools to repair the damage we have caused. We may have gone many years not even realizing the damage our anger has caused. Our anger can cause damage within our immediate relationships but our relationship with God can also be affected by our anger.

For some of us the anger itself can create a feeling of disconnect between us and God.

Keeping in mind this separation is of our own doing, God does not leave us when we get angry. Rather it is us who take our eyes off of Him.

In Deuteronomy 31:6 God challenges his people to be strong and courageous and to not fear or be in dread, he reassures us that he goes with us and he will not leave us.

When we do not take the necessary pause to process the information that is triggering us and we will often react negatively. When we react negatively, we can experience a feeling of disconnected from ourselves, God and others.

Be strong and courageous. Do not fear or be in dread of them, for it is the Lord your God who goes with you. He will not leave you or forsake you." - Deuteronomy 31:6

A hot-tempered man/woman must pay the penalty; if you rescue him, you will have to do it again." -Proverbs 19:19

This "penalty" or consequence of being hot-tempered almost always requires us to make amends to the people that were on the receiving end of our outbursts.

Reacting to an external trigger and becoming hot-tempered or angry can cause people to say hurtful things or behave in a hurtful manner and can cause damage to relationships. It wasn't until I found freedom from feeling and being angry all the time that my relationship with others began to change. When I was angry all the time my relationships suffered. My behavior was often if not always aggressive and I was difficult to talk with or to.

I can remember crying out in pain. I felt so confused and I did not want to be angry anymore. It wasn't until I became willing to change and willing to see myself clearly that I was able to find freedom from my anger. When we are open to seeing ourselves clearly and realizing how we affect the people around us, we can begin to heal.

God asks us to examine our hearts and in order to do this we have to be open and willing to make the appropriate amends to the people we have hurt. If we choose not to examine ourselves and make amends the "penalty" can be the loss of relationships and further hurt. Not to mention the feeling of being distant and/or disconnected from God may appear even greater to us.

I use to be an extremely "hot-tempered" person. I have come to realize that I had unresolved pain I had not processed and I was so unsettled emotionally. Internally everything appeared to trigger me and I was angry all the time. I did not know how to identify my emotions.

There were so many times when emotions would come up and I would push them down instead of taking the time to process them. Over the years the only emotion I seemed to express was anger.

I felt as though everything in life was happening to me. I never took the time to examine my own heart. I remember thinking it didn't matter . What I was actually saying is that I didn't matter. I didn't have the time. I just had to keep on keeping on.

I didn't know how to express myself in a healthy way. I never took the time to grieve loss or let go of pain. I was unaware that I had the power to shift my internal world and choose peace and learn to identify why there was such inner turmoil and pain.

It wasn't until I became ready to allow God into my life and became open to asking for his help in calming the rage that existed inside of me. I had so much unprocessed pain and rather than dealing with it, I allowed it to turn into anger and everyone and everything triggered me.

I have since learned how to care for my emotional wellbeing. I began to process my pain and accept responsibility for my thoughts, feelings and actions. I also learned the importance of having and setting healthy boundaries in my life.

As I began to practice these healthy rhythms my perspective and the way I viewed life began to shift. I begin to heal and I was finally able let go of the pain.

Learning new healthy rhythms in life takes practice. I had been avoiding dealing with my emotions for most of my adult life. I was not ready to surrender all the pain I had been carrying. Thankfully, with Gods help I have come a long way. I have yet to master my internal world and I can still get triggered from time to time. But the tools in this workbook have helped me and equipped me to better deal with anger when it comes, so that I am less likely to lash out.

And on the occasions where I do lash out, I am able to acknowledge my reaction and examine my heart and see what may have triggered me and genuinely apologize. I have come to deeply value the inner peace that I have in my life. The only person that can rob me of this inner peace is me. Learning to care for my emotional health has been extremely important in my life.

If you are reading this workbook, I want to say thank you. Learning to care for your emotional health is a big deal. If you are anything life me, you have been running from your emotions for years.

Please know you are not alone. There is hope.

Chapter 1

THE CALM BEFORE THE STORM

LEARNING TO MANAGE ANGER EFFECTIVELY

The Calm before the Storm

LEARNING TO MANAGE ANGER EFFECTIVELY

In this first session, we will go over a general overview of the anger management material. This includes: the purpose of the material, definitions of anger and aggression, myths about anger, anger as a habitual response, and the introduction of the anger meter, and journal we will use to learn how to monitor anger.

The workbook can be used a "self-help" book that you use on your own, it can be used with a coach/counselor for additional support, or in a group setting. The Leaders Guide Section is at the end of the workbook.

The Purpose of this workbook:

- To create a safe place for individuals to examine their relationship with anger
- Help individuals identify what triggers they may have
- Help individuals identify different queues (feelings/thoughts/actions)
- Help individuals create an anger management plan
- Develop self-control over thoughts and actions
- Develop personal strategies
- Help individuals learn manage anger effectively

As we begin to examine our relationship with anger it important to:

- **Feel Safe:** It is very important that you feel safe as you share your experiences and feelings without expressing threats of physical harm.

- **Understand Confidentiality:** What you share within this workbook and in your sessions is confidential.

- **Homework Assignments:** Doing the weekly homework assignments will improve your anger management skills and will allow you to get the most from this material.

- **Absences and Cancellations:** If you skip a week it is important to return to the workbook. If working with a coach/counselor or if attending an anger management group you should call or notify in advance if you cannot attend a session.

- **Timeouts:** A timeout is a extremely important tool to use when we begin to identify our triggers and queues. Learn to call a timeout on yourself if you feel that you may be losing control because your anger is escalating. In a group setting the group facilitator reserves the right to call a timeout at any time. Eventually, you will learn to call a timeout yourself if you feel that you may be losing control because your anger is escalating.

Definitions

In the most general sense, ***anger*** is a feeling or emotion that ranges from mild irritation to intense fury and rage. Many people often confuse anger with aggression.

Aggression is a behavior that is intended to cause harm or injury to another person or damage to property. Hostility, on the other hand, refers to a set of attitudes and judgments that motivate aggressive behaviors.

There is a type of anger of which the Bible approves, often called "righteous indignation." Righteous indignation is typically described as a reactive emotion of anger over mistreatment, insult, or malice of another. It is similar to what is called a sense of injustice. In some Christian doctrines, righteous indignation is considered the only form of anger which is not sinful.

Examples of righteous indignation can be found throughout scripture. There are scriptures where it is recorded that both God and Jesus got angry (Psalm 7:11; Mark 3:5), and where Christians are commanded to not be angry (Ephesians 4:26).

God is an honest judge. He is angry with the wicked every day. – Psalm 7:11

He looked around at them in anger and, deeply distressed at their stubborn hearts, said to the man, "Stretch out your hand." He stretched it out, and his hand was completely restored. – Mark 3:5

In your anger do not sin"[a]: Do not let the sun go down while you are still angry. – Ephesians 4:26

Additional examples of biblical anger include when David became upset over hearing Nathan the prophet sharing about an injustice (2 Samuel 12) and Jesus' anger over how some of the Jews had defiled worship at God's temple in Jerusalem (John 2:13-18). Notice that neither of these examples of anger involved self- defense, but a defense of others or of a principle.

Anger vs. Aggression

Before you learned these definitions, did you ever confuse anger with aggression? Please explain how.

When does anger become a problem?

Anger becomes a problem when it is felt too intensely, is felt too frequently, or is expressed inappropriately.

Feeling anger too intensely or frequently places extreme physical strain on the body and can create a feeling of separation within ourselves and God.

Anger can create what feels like a strain within ourselves, and our relationship with God and others.

List some ways anger may be affecting you; physically, emotionally, and/or spiritually.

1.

2.

3.

4.

5.

Payoffs & Consequences

The inappropriate expression of anger initially has apparent payoffs (e.g. releasing tension, controlling people, pushing people away, not dealing with a situation). In the long-term, however, these payoffs lead to negative consequences.

That is why they are called "apparent" payoffs; the long-term negative consequences far outweigh the short-term gains.

List some payoffs to using anger that you are familiar with (feeling of release, winning an argument, getting your way):

1.

2.

3.

4.

5.

Payoffs & Consequences
continued

He stilled the storm to a whisper; the waves of the sea were hushed.
-Psalm 107:29 (NIV)

Have you experienced any negative consequences?

List the negative consequences that you have experienced as a result of expressing your anger inappropriately (ex. loss of relationship, added stress, legal consequences etc.):

1.

2.

3.

4.

5.

Myths about Anger

Myth #1: Anger is always sin.

Many people believe that all anger is sin, when in fact there is a type of anger of which the Bible approves, often called "righteous indignation."

God is angry (Psalm 7:11; Mark 3:5), and believers are commanded to be angry (Ephesians 4:26).

Two Greek words in the New Testament are translated as "anger." One means "passion, energy" and the other means "agitated, boiling."

Biblical, anger is God-given energy. It is intended to help us not harm us.

Myth #2: Anger Is Inherited.

One misconception or myth about anger is that the way people express anger is inherited and cannot be changed. Evidence from research studies, however, indicates that people are not born with set and specific ways of expressing anger.

Rather, these studies show that the expression of anger is learned behavior and that more appropriate ways of expressing anger can also be learned.

Myth #3: Anger Automatically Leads to Aggression.

A related myth involves the misconception that the only effective way to express anger is through aggression.

There are other more constructive and assertive ways, however, to express anger. Effective anger management involves controlling the escalation of anger by learning to be more assertive rather than aggressive, changing negative and hostile "self-talk," challenging irrational beliefs, and employing a variety of behavioral strategies.

These skills, techniques, and strategies will be discussed in later sessions.

Myth #4: You Must Be Aggressive to Get What You Want.

Many people confuse assertiveness with aggression. The goal of aggression is to dominate, intimidate, harm, or injure another person—to win at any cost.

Conversely, the goal of assertiveness is to express feelings of anger in a way that is respectful of other people. Expressing yourself in an assertive manner does not blame or threaten other people and minimizes the chance of emotional harm. You will learn about the topic of assertiveness skills in more detail in sessions 7 and 8.

Myth #5: Venting Anger Is Always Desirable.

For many years, there was a popular belief that the aggressive expression of anger, such as screaming or beating on pillows, was therapeutic and healthy.

Research studies have found, however, that people who vent their anger aggressively simply get better at being angry. In other words, venting anger in an aggressive manner reinforces aggressive behavior.

Before our discussion, did you believe any of these myths about anger to be true?

ANGER IS A HABIT

Anger can become a routine, familiar, and predictable response to a variety of situations.

When anger is displayed frequently and aggressively, it can become a maladaptive habit. A habit, by definition, means performing behaviors automatically, over and over again, without thinking. The frequent and aggressive expression of anger can be viewed as a maladaptive habit because it results in negative consequences.

Has anger become a habit for you? How?

1.

2.

3.

4.

5.

ANGER IS A HABIT

continued

In what ways has anger been maladaptive (ex. easily triggered, used to bully others to get our way, as a defense mechanism when feelings are hurt).

1.

2.

3.

4.

5.

Breaking the Habit

You can break the anger habit by becoming aware of the events and circumstances that trigger your anger and the negative consequences that result from it.

In addition, you can begin to develop a set of strategies to effectively manage your anger. There is more about anger strategies in the next section.

List some anger control strategies that you might know or that you may have used in the past (counting to 10, screaming into a pillow, venting to others, etc.):

1.

2.

3.

4.

5.

Weekly Anger Meter

A simple way to monitor your anger is to use a 1 to 10 scale called the anger meter.

A score of 1 on the anger meter represents a complete lack of anger or a total state of calm, whereas 10 represents an angry and explosive loss of control that leads to negative consequences.

For each day of the upcoming week, utilize the anger meter and weekly journal page to monitor and write about where you were on the scale for each day. Begin to identify your patterns with anger. Becoming self aware is the first step in learning how to manage our anger in a healthy way.

If you are meeting with a coach/counselor or in a group be open to sharing your weekly anger meter and journal process. If you are going through this workbook on your own, you may find if beneficial to share with a trusted friend.

This is a process not a race. As you begin to learn new habits and break old habits remember it takes time and practice.

YOU ARE WORTH IT!

Along the way make sure to:

- Be KIND to yourself and others
- Give GRACE to yourself and others
- Remember NOONE is perfect
- If you, loose it and get angry, remember to BREATHE
- If or when your emotions cause you to react negatively, it is important to look back and see what happened and what you could of done differently and what you can do better in the future
- Remember you are in control of your actions and reactions

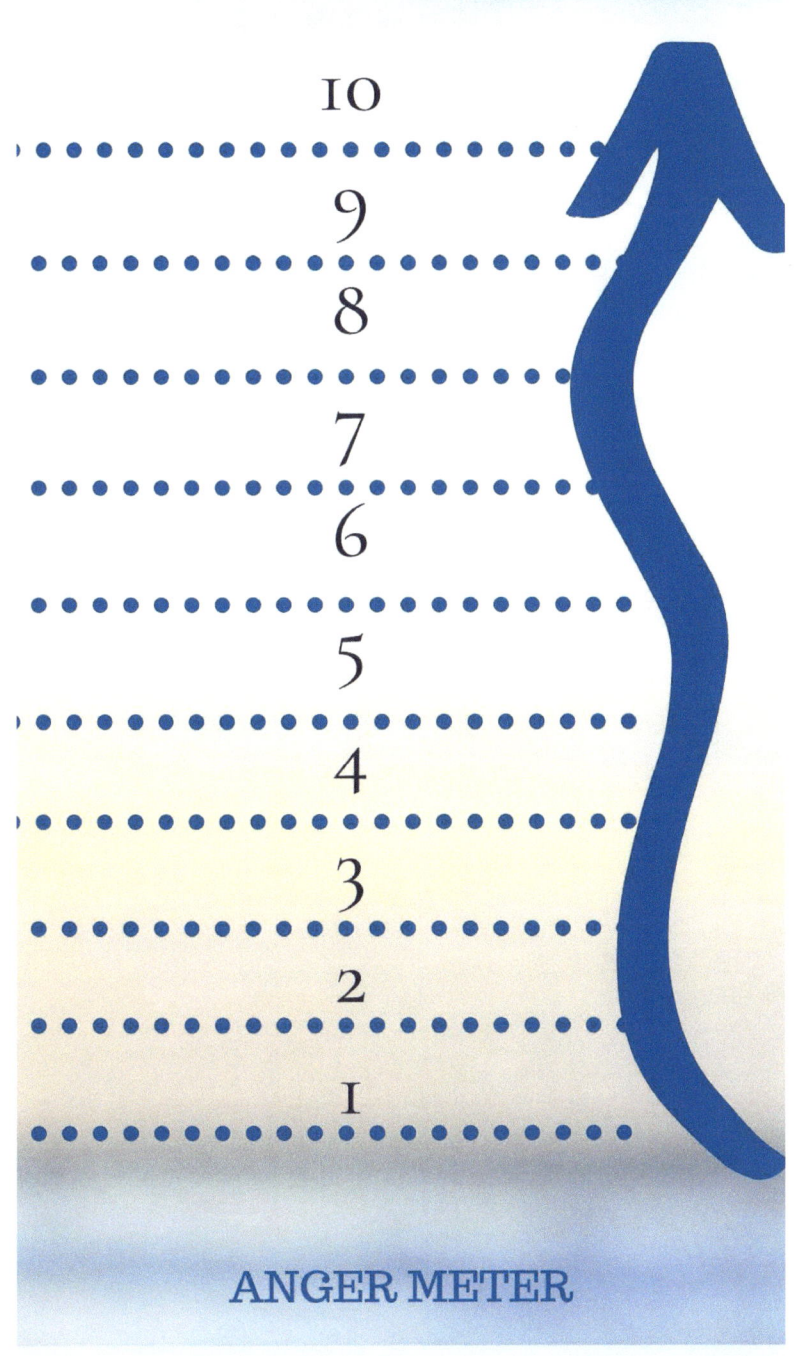

Anger Meter

A simple way to monitor your anger is to use a 1 to 10 scale called the anger meter.

A score of 1 on the anger meter represents a complete lack of anger or a total state of calm, whereas 10 represents an angry and explosive loss of control that leads to negative consequences.

For each day of the upcoming week, monitor and record the highest number you reach on the anger meter.

At the end of each chapter there is an anger meter and a weekly journal section to record your daily meter number. Begin to notice any triggers that may have come up.

It is also important to write about any strategies you used to work through your anger and what the outcome(s) were.

You have a choice.

Remember you have a choice. This workbook will help you as you begin to examine your anger on a daily basis. In the following chapters you will be learning about what your triggers are and the different types of queues that are connected to your anger. You will begin to learn that you have a choice.

Do not allow your anger to control you. Utilize the tools you will be learning with in these pages.

What are some things you have found helpful in maintaining a sence of calmness in the middle of an anger storm?

1.

2.

3.

"Sometimes God calms the storm, but sometimes God lets the storm rage and calms His child." - Leslie Gould, The Amish Nanny

Chapter 2

THE WAVES ARE RISING

LOOKING AT AN EPISODE OF ANGER

When you can't control what is happening, challenge yourself to control the way you respond to what is happening. That is where your power is.

Events and Ques

In this session, you begin to learn how to analyze an episode of anger. This involves learning how to identify events and cues that indicate an escalation of anger.

Events that trigger anger

When we get angry, often it is because we have encountered an event that has triggered our anger. Many times, these specific events touch on sensitive areas in our lives.

These sensitive areas usually refer to long-standing issues that have easily lead to anger. Maybe we have learned to anticipate getting angry when these events happen. But what about events that happen in the here an now. How do we react in those moments? What about when we remember an event from our past that made us angry and just thinking about a past event seems to make us angry all over again. It can be an endless cycle.

Here are examples of events/situations that can trigger anger:

- Long waits at a scheduled appointment
- Traffic
- Confined spaces
- A friend joking about a sensitive topic
- A friend not paying back money owed to you
- Being wrongly accused
- Clean up someone else's mess
- Having an untidy roommate
- A co-worker who lets you do all the work
- Having a neighbor who plays the stereo too loud
- Being placed on hold for long periods of time while on the telephone
- Having money or property stolen from you

Events and Ques

continued

Do you have other examples of events/situations that seem to trigger anger?

1.

2.

3.

4.

5.

Events and Ques

continued

Cues to Anger: Four cue categories

Another helpful way to monitor anger is to identify the cues that occur in response to the anger-provoking event (i.e. trigger). These cues serve as warning signs that we have become angry and that our anger is escalating. Cues can be broken down into four cue categories: physical, behavioral, emotional, and cognitive (or thought) cues.

After each category, list the cues that you have noticed when you get angry.

- **Physical Cues** (how your body responds, e.g., with an increased heart rate, tightness in the chest, feeling hot or flushed):

_____

_____

_____

_____

- **Behavioral Cues** (what you do; e.g., clench your fists, raise your voice, stare at others):

_____

_____

_____

_____

People with understanding control their anger; a hot temper shows great foolishness.
- Proverbs 14: 29 NLT

Events and Ques

continued

- **Emotional Cues** (other feelings that may occur along with anger; e.g., fear, hurt, jealousy, disrespect):

  _____

  _____

  _____

  _____

- **Cognitive Cues** (what you think about in response to the event, e.g., hostile self-talk, images of aggression and revenge):

  _____

  _____

  _____

  _____

Be not quick in your spirit to become angry, for anger lodges in the heart of fools.
−Ecclesiastes 7:9

Check-in Procedure

Monitoring Anger for the Week.

In this chapter we will began learning how to monitor anger and how to identify anger-provoking events and situations.

Each chapter going forward will have a **Check in Procedure** at the end of the material. Practice utilizing the tools every day.

Begin to recognize patterns and learn to identify what is working in helping release and manage our anger. Reflect on the highest level of anger that was reached on the anger meter each day during the week.

Identify any events that triggered anger, take note of any cues that were associated with the anger, and begin to form the strategies that are the most helpful to manage the anger in response to the event.

Begin each new chapter with the following check in sequence:

1. What was the highest number reached on the anger meter during the past week?

2. What was the event that triggered an anger response?

3. What cues were associated with the anger-provoking event?

4. What strategies were used to avoid reaching 10 on the anger meter?

Slowness to anger makes for deep understanding; a quick-tempered person stockpiles stupidity. A sound mind makes for a robust body, but runaway emotions corrode the bones. You insult your Maker when you exploit the powerless; when you're kind to the poor, you honor God. - Proverbs 14:29-31 Msg

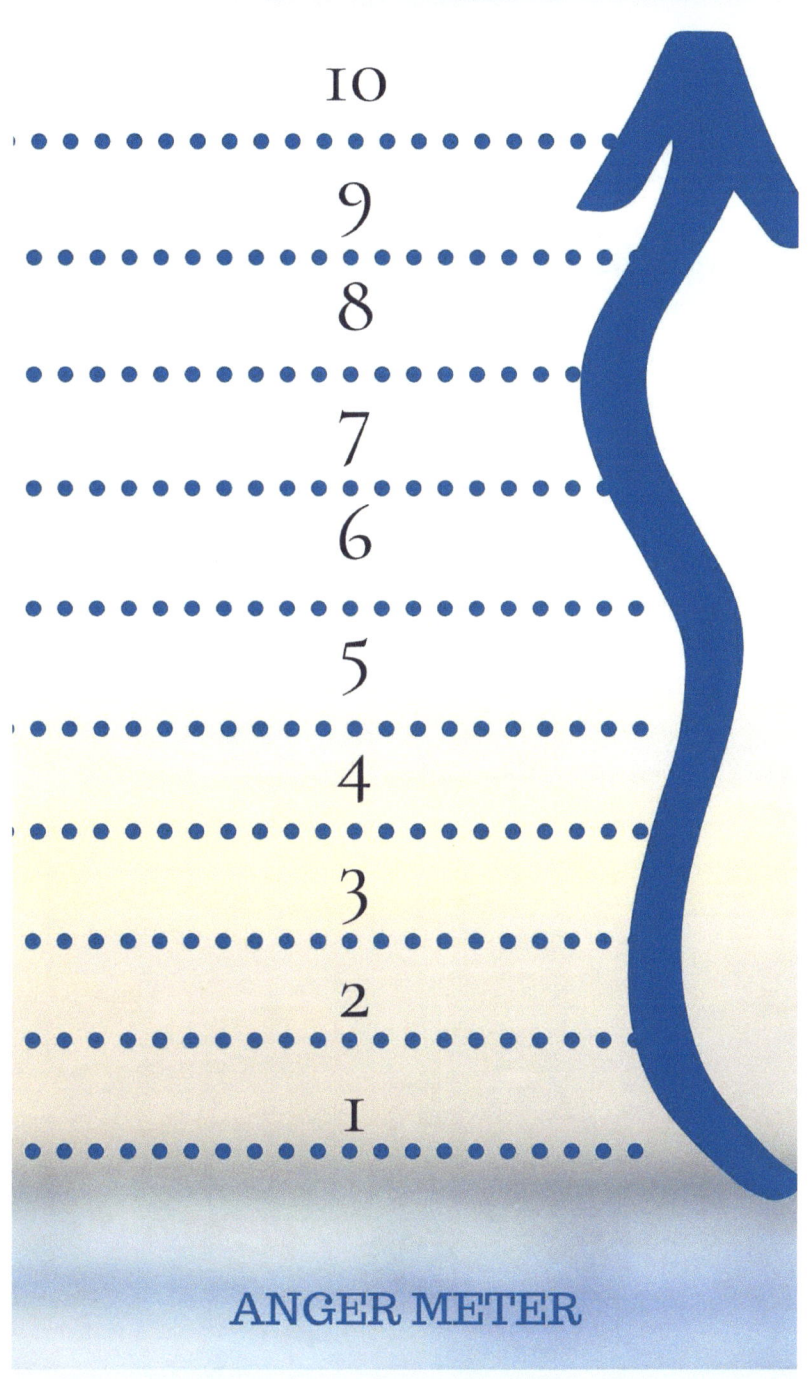

Anger Meter

A simple way to monitor your anger is to use a 1 to 10 scale called the anger meter.

A score of 1 on the anger meter represents a complete lack of anger or a total state of calm, whereas 10 represents an angry and explosive loss of control that leads to negative consequences.

For each day of the upcoming week, monitor and record the highest number you reach on the anger meter.

At the end of each chapter there is an anger meter and a weekly journal section to record your daily meter number. Begin to notice any triggers that may have come up.

It is also important to write about any strategies you used to work through your anger and what the outcome(s) were.

For each day of the week, monitor and record the highest number you reach on the anger meter.

Monday

Turesday

Wedensday

Thursday

Friday

Saturday

Sunday

Check in Procedure
continued

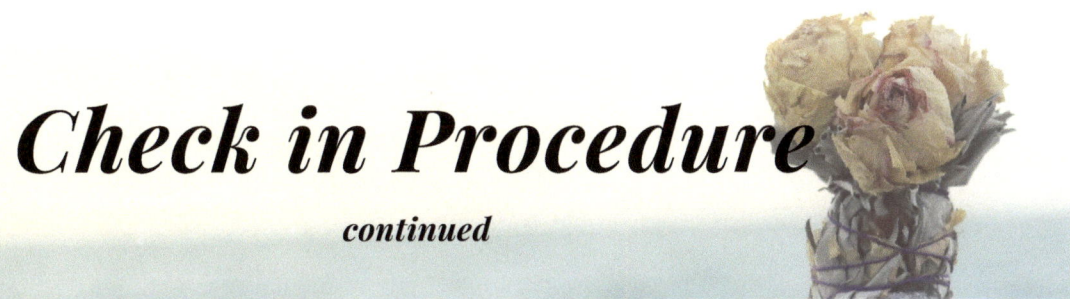

What where your physical cues:

What where your behavioral cues:

What where your cognitive cues:

Events, Cues and Strategies, identified during the check in procedure.

Ask yourself the following questions. Use the space below to see the progression as well as strategies in preventing acting out negatively in anger.

Question 1: What are my cues when I am becoming angry?

Question 2: What events appear to be triggers for me?

Question 3: What are some of strategies that are helpful in avoiding reaching an anger level that causes me to act out negatively?

Chapter 3

THE PLAN

FAILING TO PLAN IS THE SAME THINGS AS PLANNING TO FAIL.

Anger Control Plans

In this chapter, we will begin learning about specific strategies to manage your anger. The anger control plan refers to the list of strategies used to identify and manage, and control anger.

Anger Control Plans

Up to now we have been focusing on how to monitor anger.

Frist we learned how to use the anger meter to rate our anger, then we learned how to identify the events that trigger our anger and identify the physical, behavioral, emotional, and cognitive cues associated with each event.

Now we will begin to develop an anger control plan and learn how we can use specific strategies, such as timeouts and relaxation, to control anger. Some people refer to their anger control plan as their toolbox and the specific strategies used to control their anger as the tools in their toolbox.

An effective set of strategies for controlling anger should include both immediate and preventive strategies. Examples of immediate strategies include timeouts, deep- breathing exercises, and thought stopping. Examples of preventive strategies include developing an exercise program and changing irrational beliefs.

Timeouts

A timeout is a basic anger management strategy that should be in everyone's anger control plan. I think we associate a time out with a child throwing a temper tantrum, however they are quite useful if utilized prior to an emotional outburst.

A timeout can be used formally or informally. In its simplest form, it means pausing and taking a few deep breaths. This pause allows us to take some time to think instead of reacting.

It may also mean leaving the situation or conversation that may be triggering before it causes an escalation of emotion. It is okay to say, I am feeling myself getting upset, I would like to take a few moments, can we come back to this?

Anger Control Plans

The formal use of a timeout involves our relationships with other people. These relationships may involve family members, friends, and coworkers. The formal use of a timeout involves having an agreement, or a prearranged plan, by which any of the parties involved can call a timeout.

The person calling the timeout can leave the situation, if necessary. It is agreed in advance, however, that he or she will return to either finish the discussion or postpone it, depending on whether the parties involved feel they can successfully resolve the issue.

A timeout is important because it can be used effectively in the heat of the moment. Even if a person's anger is escalating quickly (as measured on the anger meter), he or she can prevent reaching 10 by taking a timeout and leaving the situation.

A timeout is also effective when used with other strategies. For example, you can take a timeout and go for a walk. You can also take a timeout and call a trusted friend or family member or write in your journal. These other strategies help you calm down during your timeout period.

Can you think of situations where you would use the timeout strategy?

Please describe them:

_____

_____

_____

_____

_____

_____

_____

Anger Control Plans

Can you think of specific strategies that you might use to control your anger?

Please describe them:

_____

_____

_____

_____

_____

_____

Sample of an Anger Control Plan

Anger Control Plan

- Take a timeout (formal or informal)
- Talk to a friend (someone you trust)
- Use the Conflict Resolution Model to express anger
- Exercise (take a walk, go to the gym, etc.)
- Attend accountability meetings
- Explore primary feelings beneath the anger

If the anger of the ruler rises against you, do not leave your place, for calmness will lay great offenses to rest. -Ecclesiastes 10:4

breathe

Relaxation through Breathing

End this chapter by practicing a deep-breathing exercise as a relaxation technique. You can practice this exercise on your own by focusing on your breathing. Take several breaths. Try to release any tension you might have in your body. You should practice this exercise as often as possible.

Here are the directions:

Find a comfortable position in your chair. Read through all of the directions.

If you would like, close your eyes; if not, just gaze down at the floor. Take a few moments to settle yourself. Now become aware of your body. Check for any tension, beginning with your feet, moving upward to your head. Notice any tension you might have in your legs, stomach, hands and arms, shoulders, neck, and face.

Try to let go of any tension.

Now, become aware of your breathing. Pay attention to your breath as it enters and leaves your body. This can be very relaxing. Notice as you inhale, does your abdomen expand (go out) or retract (go in)? Now do the same when you exhale, does you abdomen expand (go out) or retract (go in)?

Take a deep breath, slowly count to four. Notice your lungs and chest expand and rise. Now slowly exhale through your nose, slowly and notice how your chest and lungs deflate and lower.

Again, take a deep breath. Fill your lungs and your chest. Notice how much air you can take in. Hold it for a second. Now release it and exhale slowly. Inhale slowly and fully one more time.

Hold it for a second, and release.

breathe
conttunied

Continue breathing in this way for another couple of minutes. Continue to focus on your breath. With each inhalation and exhalation, feel your body becoming more and more relaxed.

Use your breathing to wash away any remaining tension.

Continue to be aware of your breath as it fills your lungs. Once more, inhale fully, hold it for a second, and release.

When you feel that you are ready, open your eyes. How was that?

Did you notice any new sensations while you were breathing? How do you feel now?

This breathing exercise can be shortened to just three deep inhalations and exhalations.

Even that can be effective in helping you relax when your anger is escalating. You can practice this at home, at work, on the bus, while waiting for an appointment, or even while walking.

The key to using deep-breathing as an effective relaxation technique is to practice it frequently and to apply it in a variety of situations.

And let the peace of Christ rule in your hearts, to which indeed you were called in one body. And be thankful. -Colossians 3:15

Check-in Procedure

Monitoring Anger for the Week

In this chapter, we began to learn how to monitor our anger and learn how to identify anger-provoking events and situations.

Each chapter has Check-In Procedure following the material.

This is a time to review:

- how we experienced anger
- what level of anger we reached on the anger meter
- identify event(s) that triggered anger
- what cues were associated with the anger
- what strategies were used to manage the anger
- what if anything we can do moving forward

Begin to recognize the events that triggered anger and the cues that you were experiencing when you felt angry.

What can happen when you do not follow the anger plan:

- EXPLOSION
- VIOLENCE
- LOSS OF CONTROL
- NEGATIVE CONSEQUENCES
- YOU LOSE!

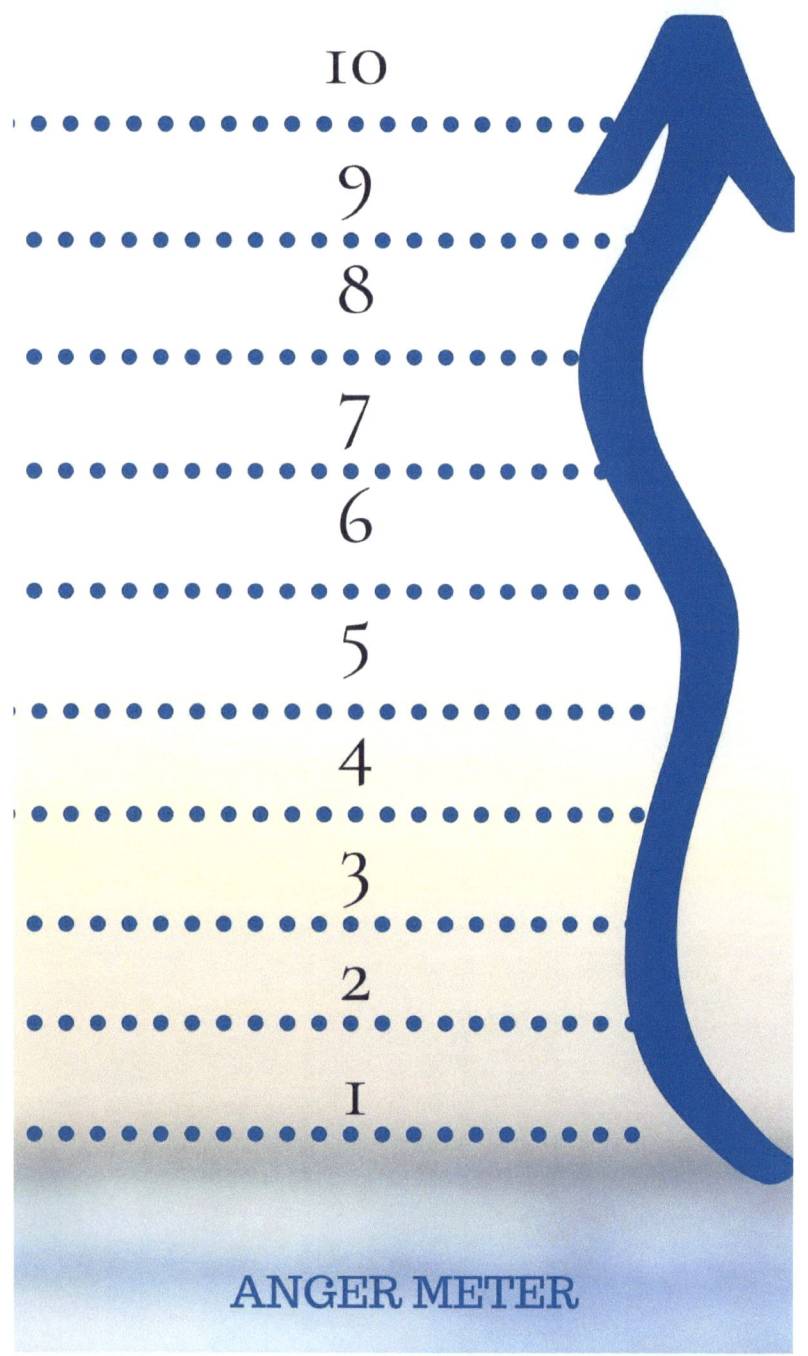

Anger Meter

A simple way to monitor your anger is to use a 1 to 10 scale called the anger meter.

A score of 1 on the anger meter represents a complete lack of anger or a total state of calm, whereas 10 represents an angry and explosive loss of control that leads to negative consequences.

For each day of the upcoming week, monitor and record the highest number you reach on the anger meter.

At the end of each chapter there is an anger meter and a weekly journal section to record your daily meter number. Begin to notice any triggers that may have come up.

It is also important to write about any strategies you used to work through your anger and what the outcome(s) were.

For each day of the week, monitor and record the highest number you reach on the anger meter.

Monday

Turesday

Wedensday

Thursday

Friday

Saturday

Sunday

Check in Procedure
continued

What where your physical cues:

What where your behavioral cues:

What where your cognitive cues:

Events, Cues and Strategies identified during the check in procedure.

Ask yourself the following questions. Use the space below to review and identify what strategies are helpful in preventing acting out negatively in anger.

Question 1: What are my cues when I am becoming angry?

Question 2: What events appear to be triggers for me?

Question 3: What are some of strategies that are helpful in avoiding reaching an anger level that causes me to act out negatively?

Chapter 4

THE CYCLE

FINDING THE COURAGE TO BREAK THE CYCLE.

The Aggression Cycle

In this session, you will learn about the aggression cycle and practice progressive muscle relaxation.

The aggression cycle serves as an integrative framework that incorporates the concepts of the anger meter, cues to anger, and the anger control plan.

The Aggression Cycle

An episode of anger can be viewed as consisting of three phases: escalation, explosion, and post-explosion. Together, these three phases make up the aggression cycle. The escalation phase is characterized by cues that indicate anger is building. As you may recall, cues are warning signs, or responses, to anger-provoking events.

If the escalation phase is allowed to continue, the explosion phase will follow. The explosion phase is marked by an uncontrollable discharge of anger that is displayed as verbal or physical aggression.

The post-explosion phase is characterized by the negative consequences that result from the verbal or physical aggression displayed during the explosion phase.

These consequences may include going to jail, making restitution, being terminated from a job, being discharged from a drug treatment or social service program, losing family and loved ones, or feelings of guilt, shame, and regret.

The Aggression Cycle and the Anger Meter

Notice that the escalation and explosion phases of the aggression cycle correspond to levels or points on the anger meter. The points on the anger meter below 10 represent the escalation phase, the building up of anger. The explosion phase, on the other hand, corresponds to a 10 on the anger meter.

The Aggression Cycle
continued

A 10 on the anger meter represents when you lose control and express anger through verbal or physical aggression that leads to negative consequences.

One of the primary objectives of anger management is to prevent reaching the explosion phase.

This is accomplished by using the anger meter to monitor changing levels of anger, attending to the cues or warning signs that indicate anger is building, and using the appropriate strategies from your anger control plans to stop the escalation of anger.

If the explosion phase is prevented, the post-explosion phase will not occur and the aggression cycle will be broken.

What phase of the aggression cycle are you in if you reach a 7 on the anger meter? (escalation, explosion, and post-explosion).

What phase are you in if you reach 10 on the anger meter? (escalation, explosion, and post-explosion).

There is an example of the "Aggression Cycle" on the following page.

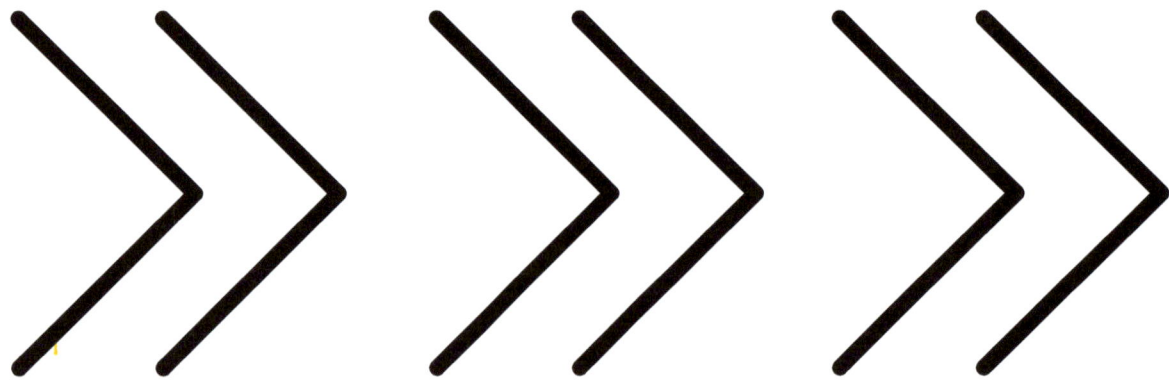

The Aggression Cycle

continued

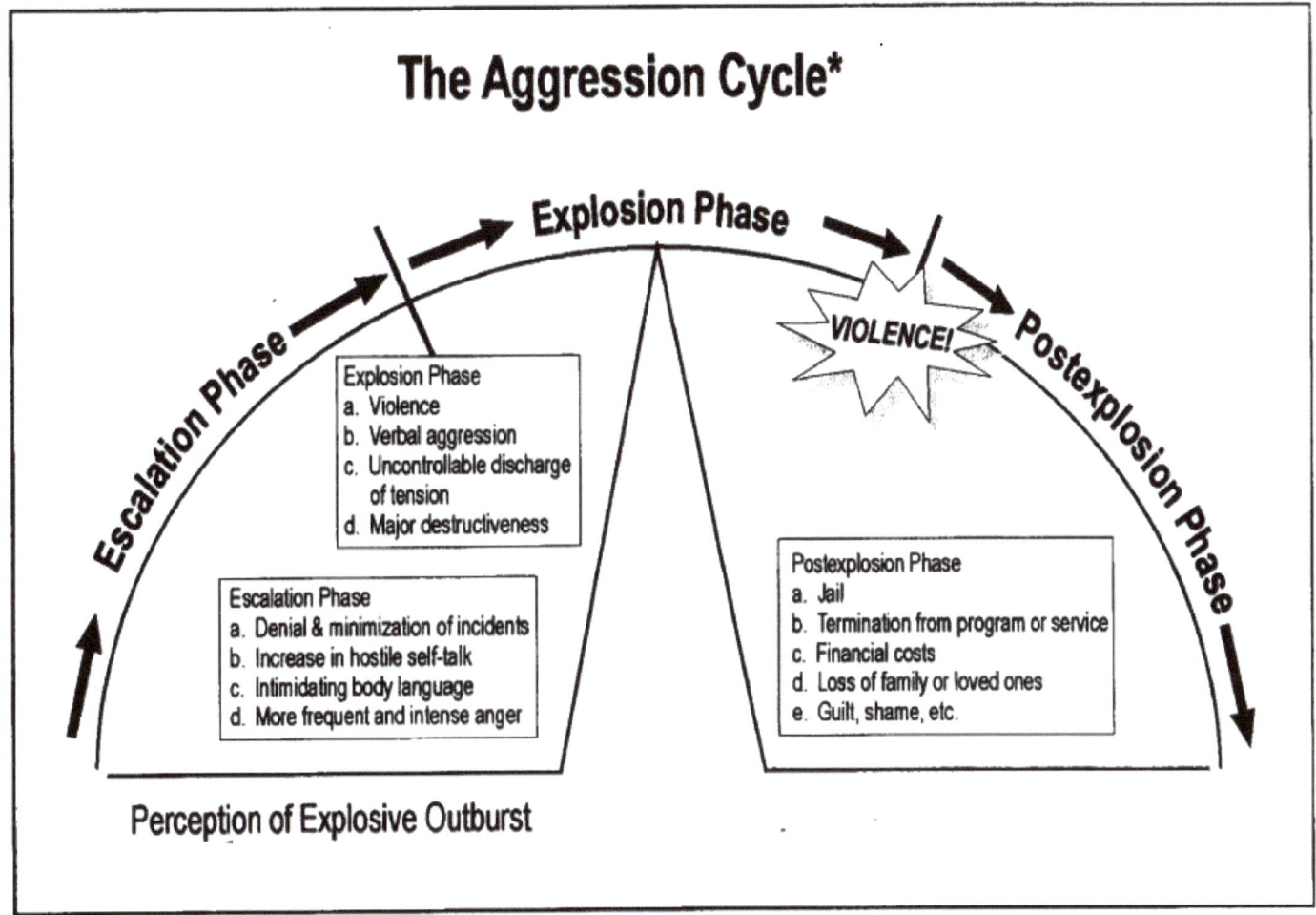

*Based on the Cycle of Violence by Lenore Walker (1979). *The Battered Woman.* New York: Harper & Row.

Relaxation through Progressive Muscle Relaxation

Last week we practiced deep-breathing as a relaxation technique. This week we are introduced to progressive muscle relaxation. This exercise should be practiced as often as possible.

Read through the directions and then begin the exercise.

Take a moment to settle in. Now, just as we did before read through the instructions first. When you are ready, begin to focus on your breathing. Take a deep breath. Hold it for a second. Now exhale fully and completely.

Again, take a deep breath. Fill your lungs and chest. Hold for a second. Now release and exhale slowly. Again, one more time, inhale slowly, hold, and release.

Now, while you continue to breathe deeply and fully, bring your awareness to your hands. Clench your fists very tightly. Hold that tension. Now relax your fists, letting your fingers unfold and letting your hands completely relax.

Again, clench your fists tightly. Hold, and release. Imagine all the tension leaving your hands down to your fingertips.

Notice the difference between tension and complete relaxation.

Now bring your awareness to your arms. Curl your arms as if you are doing a bicep curl. Tense your fists, forearms, and biceps.

Hold the tension, and release. Let your arms unfold and your hands float back to your thighs. Feel the tension drain out of your arms.

Again, curl your arms to tighten your biceps. Notice the tension, hold, and release. Let the tension flow out of your arms. Replace it with deep muscle relaxation.

Relaxation through Progressive Muscle Relaxation
continued

Now raise your shoulders toward your ears. Really tense your shoulders. Hold the tension for a second. Now gently drop your shoulders and release all the tension. Again, lift your shoulders, hold the tension, and release.

Let the tension flow from your shoulders all the way down your arms to your fingers. Notice how different your muscles feel when they are relaxed.

Now bring your awareness to your neck and your face. Tense all those muscles by making a face. Tense your neck, jaw, and forehead.

Hold the tension, and release. Let the muscles of your neck and jaw relax. Relax all the lines in your forehead.

One more time, tense all the muscles in your neck and face, hold, and release. Be aware of the muscles relaxing at the top of your head and around your eyes. Let your eyes relax in their sockets, almost as if they were sinking into the back of your head.

Relax your jaw and your throat. Relax all the muscles around your ears. Feel all the tension in your neck muscles release.

Now just sit for a few moments. Scan your body for any tension and release it. Notice how your body feels when your muscles are completely relaxed.

When you are ready, open your eyes.

Take a moment and answer following questions:

Relaxation through Progressive Muscle Relaxation
continued

1. How was that?

2. Did you notice any new sensations?

3. How does your body feel now?

4. How about your state of mind?

5. Do you notice any difference now from when you started?

Check-in Procedure

Monitoring Anger for the Week

In this chapter, we began to learn how to monitor our anger and learn how to identify anger-provoking events and situations.

Each chapter has a Check-In Procedure following the material.

This is a time to review:

how we experienced anger
what level of anger we reached on the anger meter
identify event(s) that triggered anger
what cues were associated with the anger
what strategies were used to manage the anger
what if anything we can do moving forward

Ask yourself the following questions at the end of your week:

1. What was the highest number reached on the anger meter during the past week?
2. What was the event that triggered the anger?
3. What cues were associated with the anger-provoking event?
4. What strategies were used to avoid reaching 10 on the anger meter?

What can happen when you do not follow the anger plan:

- EXPLOSION
- VIOLENCE
- LOSS OF CONTROL
- NEGATIVE CONSEQUENCES
- YOU LOSE!

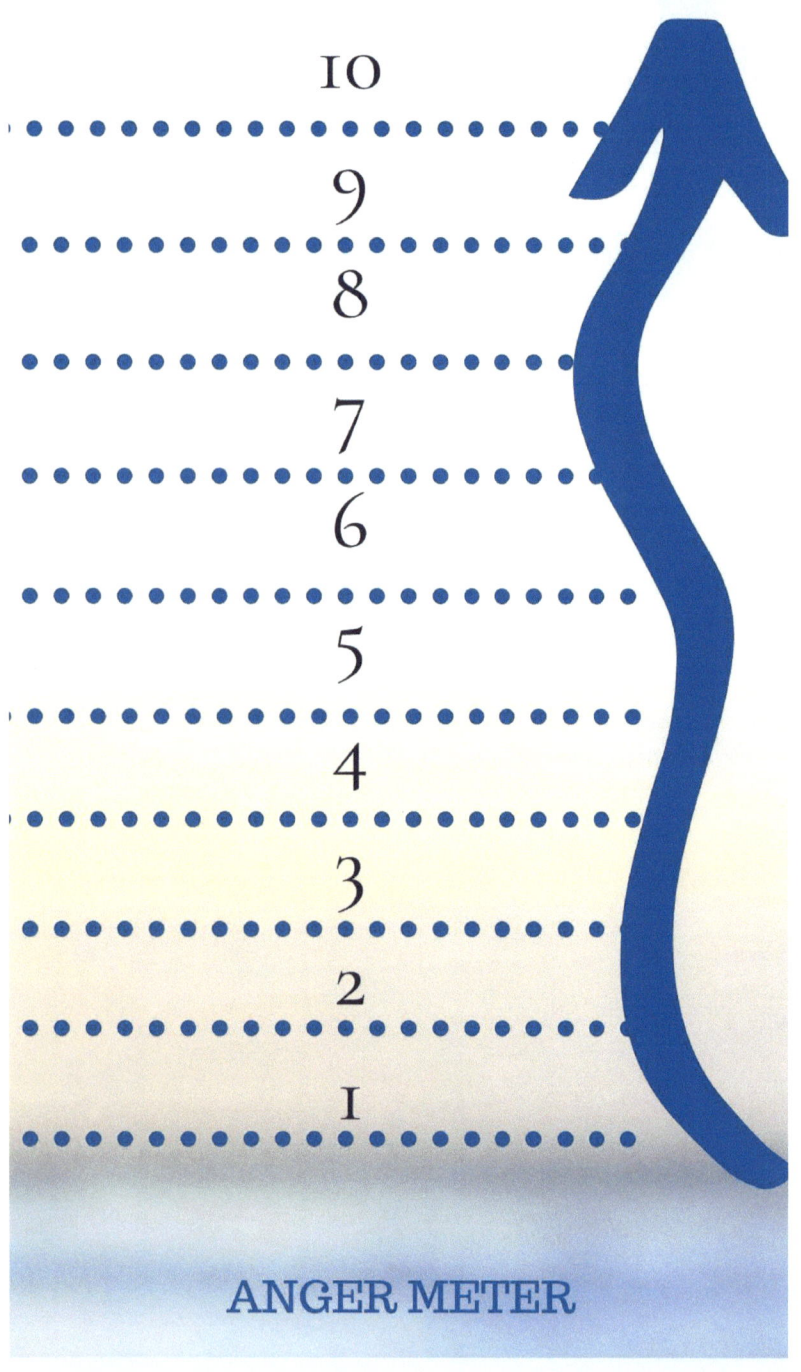

ANGER METER

Anger Meter

A simple way to monitor your anger is to use a 1 to 10 scale called the anger meter.

A score of 1 on the anger meter represents a complete lack of anger or a total state of calm, whereas 10 represents an angry and explosive loss of control that leads to negative consequences.

For each day of the upcoming week, monitor and record the highest number you reach on the anger meter.

At the end of each chapter there is an anger meter and a weekly journal section to record your daily meter number. Begin to notice any triggers that may have come up.

It is also important to write about any strategies you used to work through your anger and what the outcome(s) were.

For each day of the week, monitor and record the highest number you reach on the anger meter.

Monday

Turesday

Wedensday

Thursday

Friday

Saturday

Sunday

Check in Procedure
continued

What where your physical cues:

What where your behavioral cues:

What where your cognitive cues:

Events, Cues and Strategies identified during the check in procedure.

Ask yourself the following questions. Use the space below to review and identify what strategies are helpful in preventing acting out negatively in anger.

Question 1: What are my cues when I am becoming angry?

Question 2: What events appear to be triggers for me?

Question 3: What are some of strategies that are helpful in avoiding reaching an anger level that causes me to act out negatively?

Chapter 5

RETHINK

ONE OF THE SECRETS TO CHANGE IS RETHINKING WHAT WE THINK WE KNOW.

"A" Activating Event	"B" Beliefs	"C" Consequences	"D" Disputing
Actual Event Client's immediate interpretation of event	Evaluations Rational Irrational	Emotions Behaviours Other Thoughts Actions taken by client	Alternative belief that would lead to healthier consequences

Cognitive Restructuring

In this session, you will learn about the A-B-C-D Model as a form of cognitive restructuring.

You will also learn about thought stopping, an alternative to the A-B-C-D Model.

The A-B-C-D Model

The A-B-C-D Model (see above) is consistent with the way some people conceptualize anger management.

In this model, "**A**" stands for an activating event. The activating event is the "event" or red-flag event. "**B**" represents our beliefs about the activating event. It is not the events themselves that produce feelings such as anger; it is our interpretations and beliefs about the events. "**C**" stands for the emotional consequences. These are the feelings experienced as a result of interpretations and beliefs concerning the event. "**D**" stands for dispute.

This part of the model involves identifying any irrational beliefs and disputing the irrational beliefs with more rational or realistic ways of looking at the activating event.

The idea is to replace self-statements that lead to, or escalate, anger with statements that allow you to have a more realistic and accurate interpretation of the event.

> For every minute you are angry, you lose 60 seconds of happinesss. - Ralph Waldo Emerson

A closer look at of the A-B-C-D Model

Let's look at an example to illustrate how this works:

A = Activating Event - You've arrived at the store and as you are walking across the parking lot into the entrance when a car almost hits you. You were already feeling stressed to begin with because you had a hard time trying to find parking and you had to stay late after work.

B = Belief System - You think to yourself, "people shouldn't drive like that," "I'm a courteous driver, I don't do that," "everybody is a reckless driver," "if that car hit me, I would have been really late to pick up my kids or even worse, I could have gotten injured."

C = Consequences - After the triggering event (i.e., almost getting it), you yell an expletive out at the other driver, while giving the bird. You notice that your muscles are tense, your heart rate is high and you feel like you want to hit the something. You also notice that you feel the disconnect and maybe even some fear.

D = Dispute - In response to the triggering situation and its sequelae, rather than reinforce what's fueling the anger, you could shift your thinking (this is the "D"/dispute part of the model).

For example, you could say to yourself: "It's a bummer that some people drive recklessly, but that's just a fact of life. Most people actually are courteous drivers and I'm glad that I am as well. Who knows, maybe that driver had some emergency that they were responding to...probably not, but you never know. That was scary to almost get hit, but even the care didn't stop, I would have gotten out of the way and probably nothing drastic would have happened because of it."

As you can see, using this type of rational self-talk is likely to diffuse some of the anger and help you calm down.

Complete the following exercises on the next 2 pages.

ABCD

What does each of the letters of the A-B-C-D Model stand for?

A:

B:

C:

D:

A-B-C-D Model Worksheet

Use this cognitive-behavioral therapy (CBT) technique to help manage difficult emotions, including problems with anger management.

A=Activating Event (This refers to the initial situation or "trigger" to your strong emotion)	B=Beliefs (How you interpret the trigger: what you say to yourself about it)	C=Consequences (This how you feel and what you do in response to your belief system: the emotional and behavioral consequences that result from A + B)	D=Dispute (Examine your beliefs and expectations. Are they unrealistic or irrational? If so, what may be alternative ways to relate to the situation?)
write in each box:			

Thought Stopping

A second approach to controlling anger is called "thought stopping."

Thought stopping is an alternative to the A-B-C-D Model. In this approach, you simply tell yourself through a series of self-commands to stop thinking the thoughts that are making you angry.

For example, you might tell yourself, "I need to stop thinking these thoughts", "I will get into trouble if I continue thinking this way," or "Don't buy into this situation," or "Don't go there." In this process you can also utilize prayer and asking God to take these thoughts from you; "God please take this thought from me". you may have to do it over and over again. But I have found that if I surrender and ask for help, God shows up.

In other words, instead of trying to dispute your thoughts and beliefs as outlined in the A-B-C-D Model, the goal is to stop your current pattern of angry thoughts before they lead to an escalation of anger and a loss of control.

Another useful tool in thought stopping is placing the a rubber band technique.

1. You'll need a rubber band or elastic band. Keep it on your wrist so it is there at all times.
2. Whenever an unwanted thought enters your mind, pull the rubber band and let go, so it snaps on your wrist. You need to feel the snap but it should not leave a red mark.
3. This snaps you back from the unwanted thoughts to the present moment.
4. Next, you shout the word STOP (you can imagine saying STOP in your mind. Or say it out loud if you are alone.) Then, think of a big red stop sign. See the big letters spelling out the word STOP. See it in your mind, notice what color the word stop is.
5. Take a deep breath and take a sip of water and say that feels better.

You are giving a message to your unconscious mind so say it no matter how you feel at the moment. The unconscious part of the mind hears the message and reacts with different types of chemicals. This adds to the process of having you feel more relaxed.

What are some other examples of thought-stopping techniques and statements you can use when you become angry?

1.

2.

3.

4.

Check-in Procedure

Monitoring Anger for the Week

In this chapter, we began to learn how to monitor our anger and learn how to identify anger-provoking events and situations.

Each chapter has a Check-In Procedure following the material.

This is a time to review:

how we experienced anger
what level of anger we reached on the anger meter
identify event(s) that triggered anger
what cues were associated with the anger
what strategies were used to manage the anger
what if anything we can do moving forward

Ask yourself the following questions at the end of your week:

1. What was the highest number reached on the anger meter during the past week?
2. What was the event that triggered the anger?
3. What cues were associated with the anger-provoking event?
4. What strategies were used to avoid reaching 10 on the anger meter?

What can happen when you do not follow the anger plan:

- EXPLOSION
- VIOLENCE
- LOSS OF CONTROL
- NEGATIVE CONSEQUENCES
- YOU LOSE!

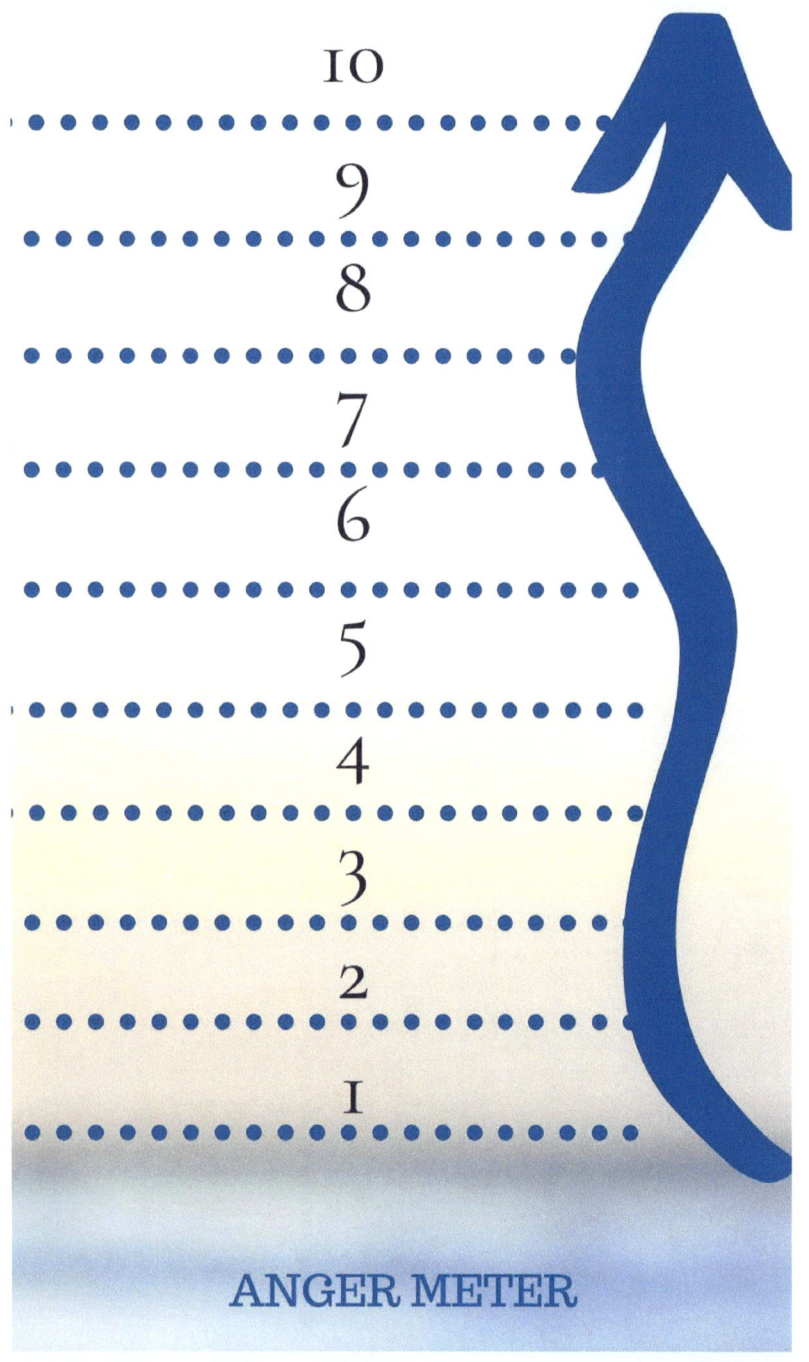

Anger Meter

A simple way to monitor your anger is to use a 1 to 10 scale called the anger meter.

A score of 1 on the anger meter represents a complete lack of anger or a total state of calm, whereas 10 represents an angry and explosive loss of control that leads to negative consequences.

For each day of the upcoming week, monitor and record the highest number you reach on the anger meter.

At the end of each chapter there is an anger meter and a weekly journal section to record your daily meter number. Begin to notice any triggers that may have come up.

It is also important to write about any strategies you used to work through your anger and what the outcome(s) were.

For each day of the week, monitor and record the highest number you reach on the anger meter.

Monday

Turesday

Wedensday

Thursday

Friday

Saturday

Sunday

Check in Procedure
continued

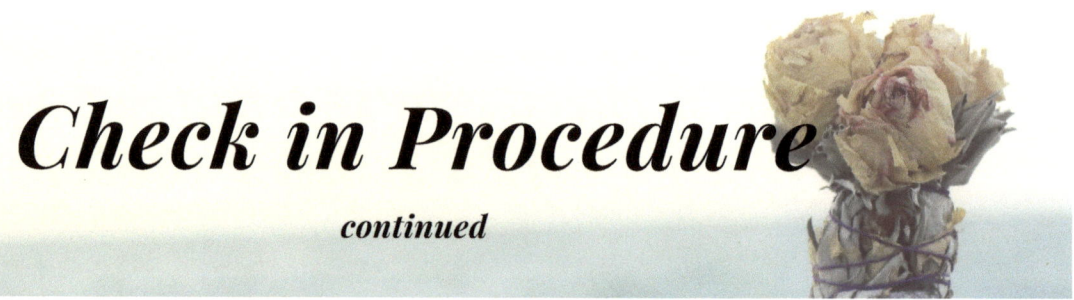

What where your physical cues:

What where your behavioral cues:

What where your cognitive cues:

Events, Cues and Strategies, identified during the check in procedure.

Ask yourself the following questions. Use the space below to see the progression as well as strategies in preventing acting out negatively in anger.

Question 1: What are my cues when I am becoming angry?

Question 2: What events appear to be triggers for me?

Question 3: What are some of strategies that are helpful in avoiding reaching an anger level that causes me to act out negatively?

Chapter 6

REVIEW

THERE IS SOMETHING ABOUT REVIEWING THE LESSONS OF
THE PAST THAT PREPARE US TO FACE
THE CHALLENGES OF THE FUTURE.
- L. TOM PERRY

Review

Review Session

In this session, we will review and summarize the basic concepts of anger management presented this far. If you have any questions or you are unclear about any of the concepts or strategies, please ask me via my email if working through this workbook on your own or ask your coach or group leader to further review this material with you.

1. What was the highest number you reached on the anger meter during the past week?
2. What was the event that triggered your anger?
3. What cues were associated with the anger-provoking event?
4. What strategies did you use to avoid reaching 10 on the anger meter?

What can happen when you do not follow the anger plan:

- EXPLOSION
- VIOLENCE
- LOSS OF CONTROL
- NEGATIVE CONSEQUENCES
- YOU LOSE!

Review

Events and Ques

Cues to Anger: Four Cue Categories

Identifying the cues that occur in response to the anger-provoking event. These cues serve as warning signs that you have become angry and that your anger is escalating. Cues can be broken down into four cue categories: physical, behavioral, emotional, and cognitive (or thought) cues.

After each category, list the cues that you have noticed when you get angry.

- **Physical Cues** (how your body responds, e.g., with an increased heart rate, tightness in the chest, feeling hot or flushed):

  _____

  _____

  _____

- **Behavioral Cues** (what you do; e.g., clench your fists, raise your voice, stare at others):

  _____

  _____

  _____

People with understanding control their anger; a hot temper shows great foolishness.
- Proverbs 14: 29 NLT

Review
Events, Cues and Strategies

Ask yourself the following questions. Use the space below to see the progression as well as strategies in preventing acting out negatively in anger.

Question 1: What are my cues when I am becoming angry?

Question 2: What events appear to be triggers for me?

Question 3: What are some of strategies that are helpful in avoiding reaching an anger level that causes me to act out negatively?

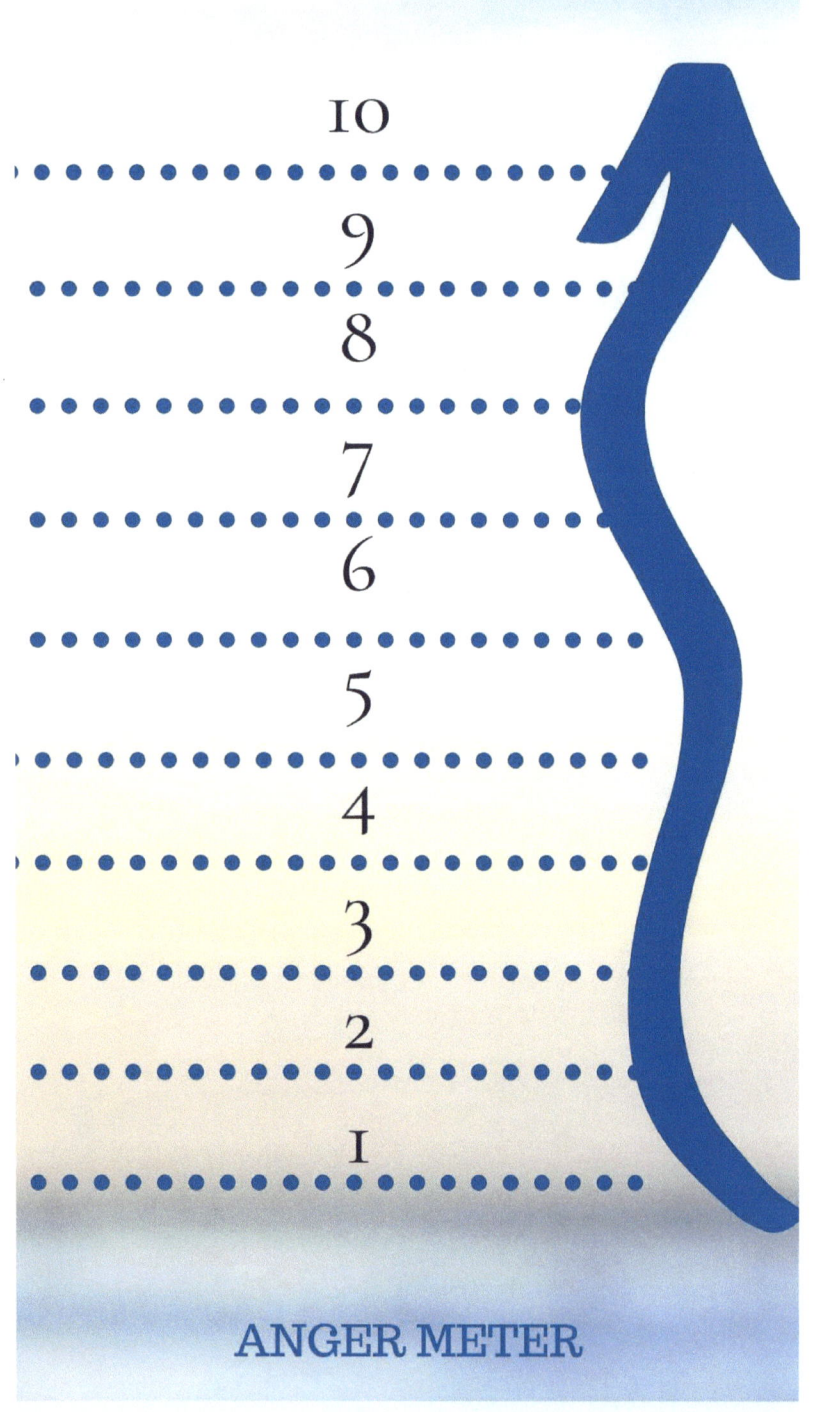

Anger Meter

A simple way to monitor your anger is to use a 1 to 10 scale called the anger meter.

A score of 1 on the anger meter represents a complete lack of anger or a total state of calm, whereas 10 represents an angry and explosive loss of control that leads to negative consequences.

For each day of the upcoming week, monitor and record the highest number you reach on the anger meter.

At the end of each chapter there is an anger meter and a weekly journal section to record your daily meter number. Begin to notice any triggers that may have come up.

It is also important to write about any strategies you used to work through your anger and what the outcome(s) were.

For each day of the week, monitor and record the highest number you reach on the anger meter.

Monday

Turesday

Wedensday

Thursday

Friday

Saturday

Sunday

Check in Procedure
continued

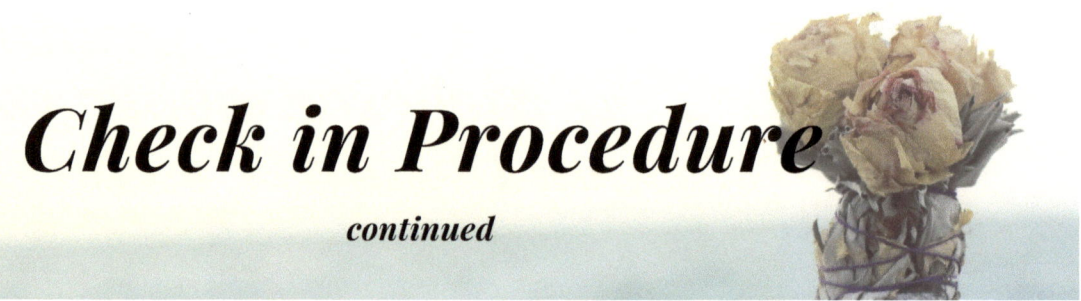

What where your physical cues:

What where your behavioral cues:

What where your cognitive cues:

Events, Cues and Strategies, identified during the check in procedure.

Ask yourself the following questions. Use the space below to see the progression as well as strategies in preventing acting out negatively in anger.

Question 1: What are my cues when I am becoming angry?

Question 2: What events appear to be triggers for me?

Question 3: What are some of strategies that are helpful in avoiding reaching an anger level that causes me to act out negatively?

Chapter's 7 & 8

ASSERTIVENESS

&

CONFLICT RESOLUTION

If another believer [a] sins against you, go privately and point out the offense. If the other person listens and confesses it, you have won that person back. -Matthew 18:15

Assertiveness & Conflict Resolution Model

In these two sessions, we will learn about assertiveness and the Conflict Resolution Model and how acting in an assertive manner can reduce conflicts you have with others.

Assertiveness Training

As you remember from chapter 1, aggression is behavior that is intended to cause harm to another person or damage to property. This behavior can include verbal abuse, threats, or violent acts. Often, the first reaction when another person has violated your rights is to fight back or retaliate. The basic message of aggression is that my feelings, thoughts, and beliefs are very important and your feelings, thoughts, and beliefs are unimportant and inconsequential.

One alternative to aggressive behavior is to act passively or in a non-assertive manner. This behavior can also have a negative effect because you allow your rights to be violated.

You may resent and become angry with the person who violated your rights, and you may also be angry with yourself for not standing up for your rights. The basic message of passivity is that your feelings, thoughts, and beliefs are very important, but my feelings, thoughts, and beliefs are unimportant and inconsequential.

From an anger management perspective, the best way to deal with a person who has violated your rights is to act assertively. Acting assertively involves standing up for your rights in such a way that is respectful of other people.

The basic message of assertiveness is that my feelings, thoughts, and beliefs are important, and your feelings, thoughts, and beliefs are equally important.

By acting assertively, you can express your feelings, thoughts, and beliefs to the person who violated your rights without suffering the negative consequences associated with aggression or the feeling of less than that is associated with passivity or non-assertion.

Assertiveness & Conflict Resolution Model

continued

It is important to emphasize that assertive, aggressive, and passive responses are learned behaviors; they are not innate, unchangeable traits.

By practicing the Conflict Resolution Model, you can learn to develop assertive responses that will allow you to manage interpersonal conflicts in a more effective way.

What are some problems that you may experience if you act aggressively during conflicts with others?

What are some problems that you may experience if you respond passively during conflicts?

What are some of the advantages of acting assertively when trying to resolve conflicts?

Assertiveness & Conflict Resolution Model

continued

Conflict Resolution Model

The Conflict Resolution Model is one method you can use to act assertively.

It involves **five steps** that can easily be memorized.

1)   Identifying the Problem. This step involves identifying the specific problem that is causing the conflict (e.g., a friend's not being on time when you come to pick him or her up).

2)   Identifying the Feelings. In this step, you identify the feelings associated with the conflict (e.g., frustration, hurt, or annoyance).

3)   Identifying the Specific Impact. This step involves identifying the specific impact or outcome of the problem that is causing the conflict (e.g., being late for the meeting that you and your friend plan to attend).

4)   Deciding Whether to Resolve the Conflict. This step involves deciding whether to resolve the conflict or let it go. In other words, is the conflict important enough to bring up?

5)   Addressing and Resolving the Conflict. In this step, you set up a time to address the conflict, describe how you perceive it, express your feelings about it, and discuss how it can be resolved.

Know this, my beloved brothers: let every person be quick to hear, slow to speak, slow to anger – James 1:19 ESV

Assertiveness & Conflict Resolution Model

continued

What is the purpose of using the Conflict Resolution Model?

Identify the five steps of the Conflict Resolution Model, and apply it to an example of your own.

1.

2.

3.

4.

5.

Check-in Procedure

Monitoring Anger for the Week.

In this session, you began to learn to monitor your anger and to identify anger-provoking events and situations.

In each weekly session, there will be a Check-In Procedure to follow up on the homework assignment from the previous week and to report the highest level of anger reached on the anger meter during the past week.

You will also be asked to identify the event that triggered your anger, the cues that were associated with your anger, and the strategies you used to manage your anger in response to the event. You will be using the following format to check in at the beginning of each session:

1) What was the highest number you reached on the anger meter during the past week?

2) What was the event that triggered your anger?

3) What cues were associated with the anger-provoking event?

4) What strategies did you use to avoid reaching 10 on the anger meter?

What can happen when you do not follow the anger plan:

- EXPLOSION
- VIOLENCE
- LOSS OF CONTROL
- NEGATIVE CONSEQUENCES
- YOU LOSE!

Check-in Procedure

continued

Cues to Anger: Four Cue Categories

Identifying the cues that occur in response to the anger-provoking event. These cues serve as warning signs that you have become angry and that your anger is escalating. Cues can be broken down into four cue categories: physical, behavioral, emotional, and cognitive (or thought) cues.

After each category, list the cues that you have noticed when you get angry.

- **Physical Cues** (how your body responds, e.g., with an increased heart rate, tightness in the chest, feeling hot or flushed):

_____

_____

_____

- **Behavioral Cues** (what you do; e.g., clench your fists, raise your voice, stare at others):

_____

_____

_____

People with understanding control their anger; a hot temper shows great foolishness.
- Proverbs 14: 29 NLT

Check-in Procedure

continued

- **Emotional Cues** (other feelings that may occur along with anger; e.g., fear, hurt, jealousy, disrespect):

  _____

  _____

  _____

- **Cognitive Cues** (what you think about in response to the event, e.g., hostile self-talk, images of aggression and revenge):

  _____

  _____

  _____

Blessed are the peacemakers, for they shall be called sons of God. –Matthew 5:9

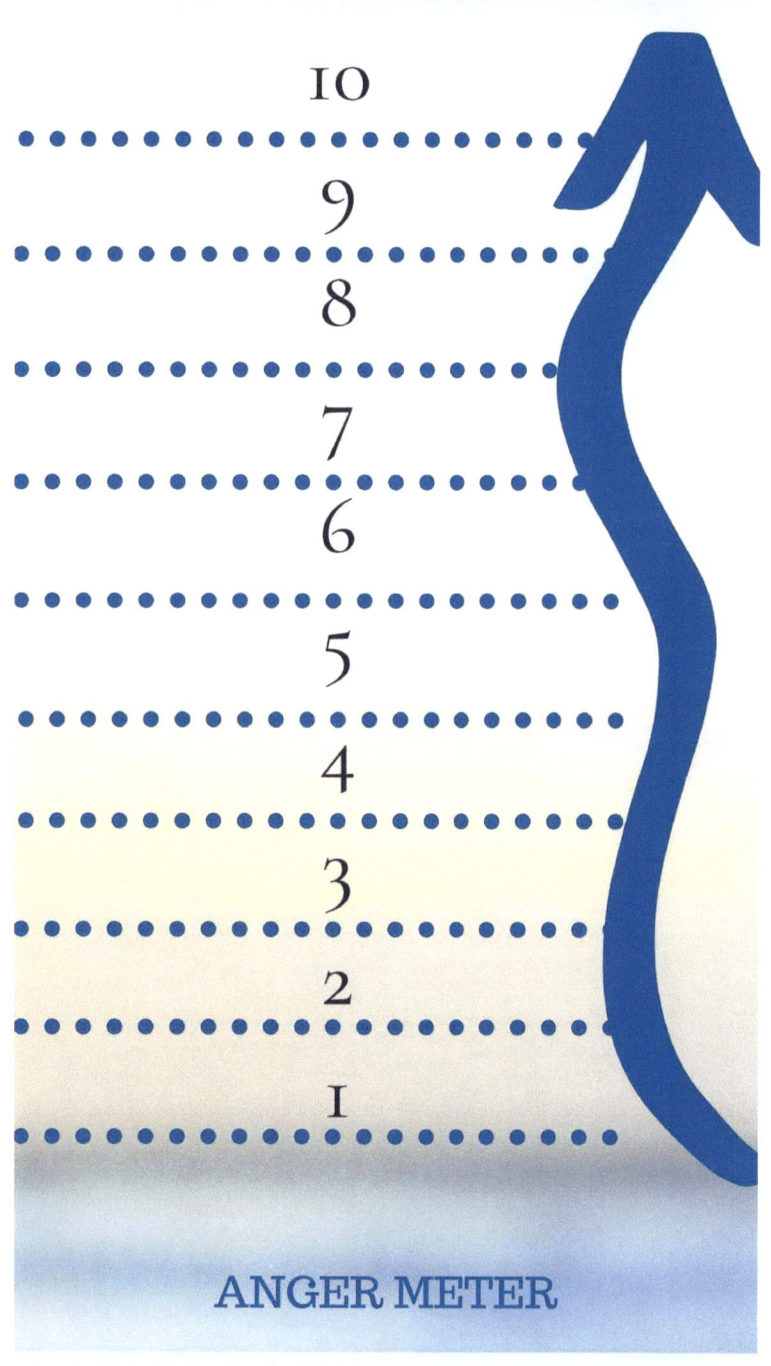

Anger Meter

A simple way to monitor your anger is to use a 1 to 10 scale called the anger meter.

A score of 1 on the anger meter represents a complete lack of anger or a total state of calm, whereas 10 represents an angry and explosive loss of control that leads to negative consequences.

For each day of the upcoming week, monitor and record the highest number you reach on the anger
meter.

At the end of each chapter there is an anger meter and a weekly journal section to record your daily meter number. Begin to notice any triggers that may have come up.

It is also important to write about any strategies you used to work through your anger and what the outcome(s) were.

For each day of the week, monitor and record the highest number you reach on the anger meter.

Monday

Turesday

Wedensday

Thursday

Friday

Saturday

Sunday

Check in Procedure
continued

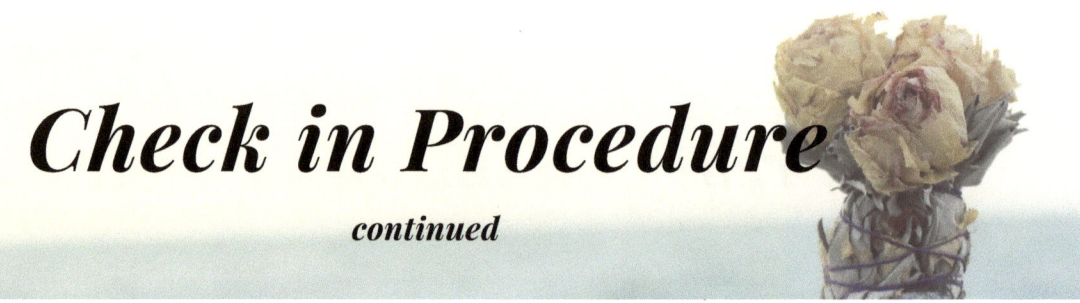

What where your physical cues:

What where your behavioral cues:

What where your cognitive cues:

Events, Cues and Strategies, identified during the check in procedure.

Ask yourself the following questions. Use the space below to see the progression as well as strategies in preventing acting out negatively in anger.

Question 1: What are my cues when I am becoming angry?

Question 2: What events appear to be triggers for me?

Question 3: What are some of strategies that are helpful in avoiding reaching an anger level that causes me to act out negatively?

Chapter's 9 & 10

HEREDITY

or

HABIT

Are we formed by where we come from or the choices we make in life?

Anger and the Family

In these two sessions, we look at how anger and other emotions were expressed in our families. This involves analyzing how past family interactions affect current thoughts, feelings, and behaviors.

For many of us, the interactions we had with our parents have strongly influenced our behaviors, thoughts, feelings, and attitudes as adults.

With regard to anger and its expression, these feelings and behaviors were usually modeled for us by our parents or parental figures. The following series of questions addresses the interactions you had with your parents and the families that you grew up in.

Discussing family issues can sometimes bring up uncomfortable feelings. Be sure to discuss these feelings with the group leader or your coach/counselor.

Question 1: Describe your family. Did you live with both parents?

Anger and the Family
continued

Question 2: Did you have any brothers and sisters? Where did you grow up?

Question 3: How was anger expressed in your family while you were growing up? How did your father express anger?

Question 4: How did your mother express anger?

Anger and the Family
continued

Question 5: Were you ever threatened with physical violence?

Question 6: Was your father abusive to your mother or you?

Question 7: How were other emotions, such as happiness and sadness, expressed in your family? Was emotional expression limited to feelings of anger and frustration, or were many different kinds of emotions expressed?

Anger and the Family
continued

Question 8: Answer question 7 below...

Question 9: How were you disciplined and by whom? Was physical punishment involved (e.g., being hit with hands, belts, switches, or other objects)? How did you respond to this discipline?

Anger and the Family

continued

Question 10: What role did you take in your family? For example, were you the hero, the rescuer, the victim, the clown, the scapegoat, etc.?

Question 11: What messages did you receive about your father and men in general? What messages did you receive about your mother and women in general?

Anger and the Family
continued

Question 11: What feelings, thoughts, and behaviors carry over into your relationships today?

Question 12: What purpose do these behaviors serve today?

Anger and the Family
continued

Question 13: What would happen if you gave up these behaviors?

Additional Notes......

Check-in Procedure

Monitoring Anger for the Week.

In this session, we learned to monitor anger and to identify anger-provoking events and situations.

In each weekly session, there will be a Check-In Procedure to follow up on the homework assignment from the previous week and to report the highest level of anger reached on the anger meter during the past week.

You will also be asked to identify the event that triggered your anger, the cues that were associated with your anger, and the strategies you used to manage your anger in response to the event. You will be using the following format to check in at the beginning of each session:

1) What was the highest number you reached on the anger meter during the past week?

2) What was the event that triggered your anger?

3) What cues were associated with the anger-provoking event?

4) What strategies did you use to avoid reaching 10 on the anger meter?

What can happen when you do not follow the anger plan:

- EXPLOSION
- VIOLENCE
- LOSS OF CONTROL
- NEGATIVE CONSEQUENCES
- YOU LOSE!

Check-in Procedure

continued

Cues to Anger: Four Cue Categories

Identifying the cues that occur in response to the anger-provoking event. These cues serve as warning signs that you have become angry and that your anger is escalating. Cues can be broken down into four cue categories: physical, behavioral, emotional, and cognitive (or thought) cues.

After each category, list the cues that you have noticed when you get angry.

- **Physical Cues** (how your body responds, e.g., with an increased heart rate, tightness in the chest, feeling hot or flushed):

_____

_____

_____

- **Behavioral Cues** (what you do; e.g., clench your fists, raise your voice, stare at others):

_____

_____

_____

People with understanding control their anger; a hot temper shows great foolishness.
- Proverbs 14: 29 NLT

Check-in Procedure

continued

- **Emotional Cues** (other feelings that may occur along with anger; e.g., fear, hurt, jealousy, disrespect):

  _____

  _____

  _____

  _____

  _____

- **Cognitive Cues** (what you think about in response to the event, e.g., hostile self-talk, images of aggression and revenge):

  _____

  _____

  _____

  _____

  _____

Blessed are the peacemakers, for they shall be called sons of God. –Matthew 5:9

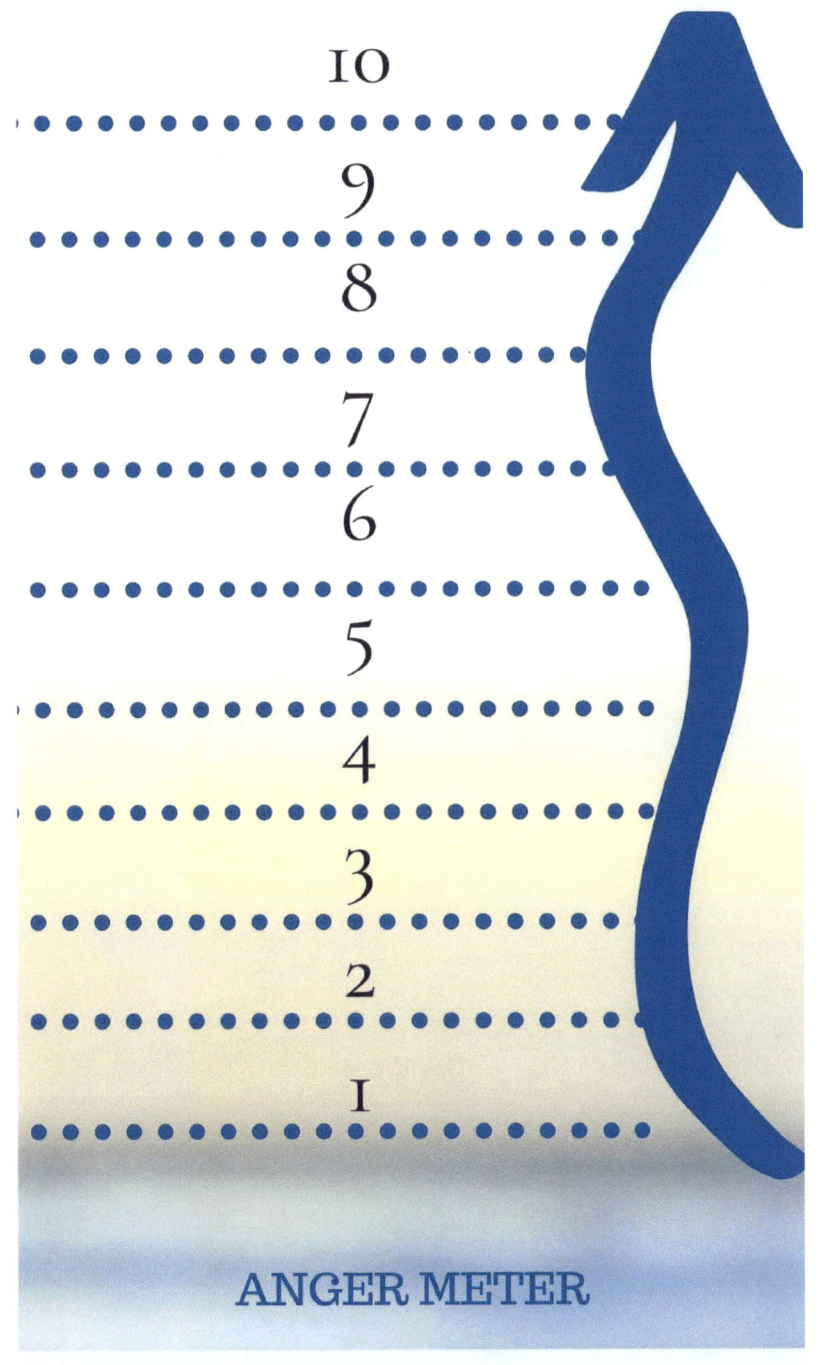

Anger Meter

A simple way to monitor your anger is to use a 1 to 10 scale called the anger meter.

A score of 1 on the anger meter represents a complete lack of anger or a total state of calm, whereas 10 represents an angry and explosive loss of control that leads to negative consequences.

For each day of the upcoming week, monitor and record the highest number you reach on the anger meter.

At the end of each chapter there is an anger meter and a weekly journal section to record your daily meter number. Begin to notice any triggers that may have come up.

It is also important to write about any strategies you used to work through your anger and what the outcome(s) were.

For each day of the week, monitor and record the highest number you reach on the anger meter.

Monday

Turesday

Wedensday

Thursday

Friday

Saturday

Sunday

Check in Procedure
continued

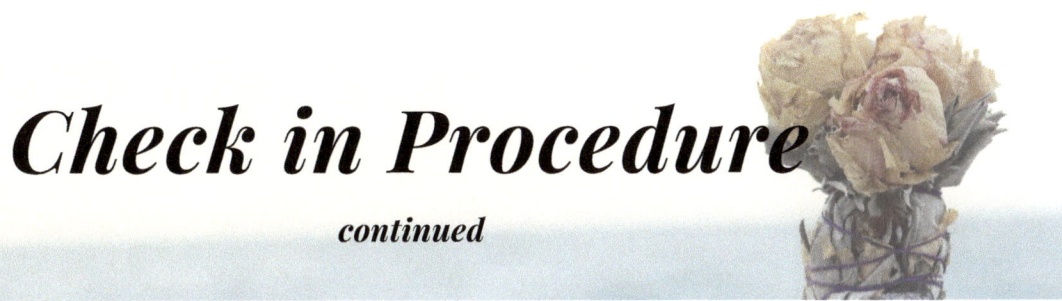

What where your physical cues:

What where your behavioral cues:

What where your cognitive cues:

Events, Cues and Strategies, identified during the check in procedure.

Ask yourself the following questions. Use the space below to see the progression as well as strategies in preventing acting out negatively in anger.

Question 1: What are my cues when I am becoming angry?

Question 2: What events appear to be triggers for me?

Question 3: What are some of strategies that are helpful in avoiding reaching an anger level that causes me to act out negatively?

Chapter 11

FINAL REVIEW

"The improvement of understanding is for two ends: first, our own increase of knowledge; secondly, to enable us to deliver that knowledge to others." – John Locke

Final Review

In this last session, we will review and summarize the basic concepts of anger management presented this far. If you have any questions or you are unclear about any of the concepts or strategies, ask for further review of any of the sessions covered.

1. What was the highest number you reached on the anger meter during the past week?
2. What was the event that triggered your anger?
3. What cues were associated with the anger-provoking event?
4. What strategies did you use to avoid reaching 10 on the anger meter?

What can happen when you do not follow the anger plan:

- EXPLOSION
- VIOLENCE
- LOSS OF CONTROL
- NEGATIVE CONSEQUENCES
- YOU LOSE!

Final Review

Events and Ques

Cues to Anger: Four Cue Categories

Identifying the cues that occur in response to the anger-provoking event. These cues serve as warning signs that you have become angry and that your anger is escalating. Cues can be broken down into four cue categories: physical, behavioral, emotional, and cognitive (or thought) cues.

After each category, list the cues that you have noticed when you get angry.

- **Physical Cues** (how your body responds, e.g., with an increased heart rate, tightness in the chest, feeling hot or flushed):

_____

_____

_____

_____

- **Behavioral Cues** (what you do; e.g., clench your fists, raise your voice, stare at others):

_____

_____

_____

_____

People with understanding control their anger; a hot temper shows great foolishness.
- Proverbs 14: 29 NLT

Final Review
Events and Ques

continued

- **Emotional Cues** (other feelings that may occur along with anger; e.g., fear, hurt, jealousy, disrespect):

  _____

  _____

  _____

  _____

  _____

- **Cognitive Cues** (what you think about in response to the event, e.g., hostile self-talk, images of aggression and revenge):

  _____

  _____

  _____

  _____

  _____

Blessed are the peacemakers, for they shall be called sons of God. –Matthew 5:9

Final Review

continued

What have you learned about your relationship with anger?

Final Review

continued

Which of the sessions really hit home for you and why?

(anger vs. aggression, payoffs and consequences, anger myths, anger is a habit, breaking the habit, events and ques, anger control plan, relaxation techniques, aggression cycle, cognitive restructuring, assertiveness and conflict resolution, heredity or habit)

_____
_____
_____
_____
_____
_____
_____
_____
_____
_____
_____
_____
_____
_____
_____
_____
_____

Final Anger Meter

Review your first anger and last anger meters below. How has your relationship to anger changed?

_____
_____
_____
_____
_____
_____
_____
_____
_____
_____
_____
_____
_____
_____

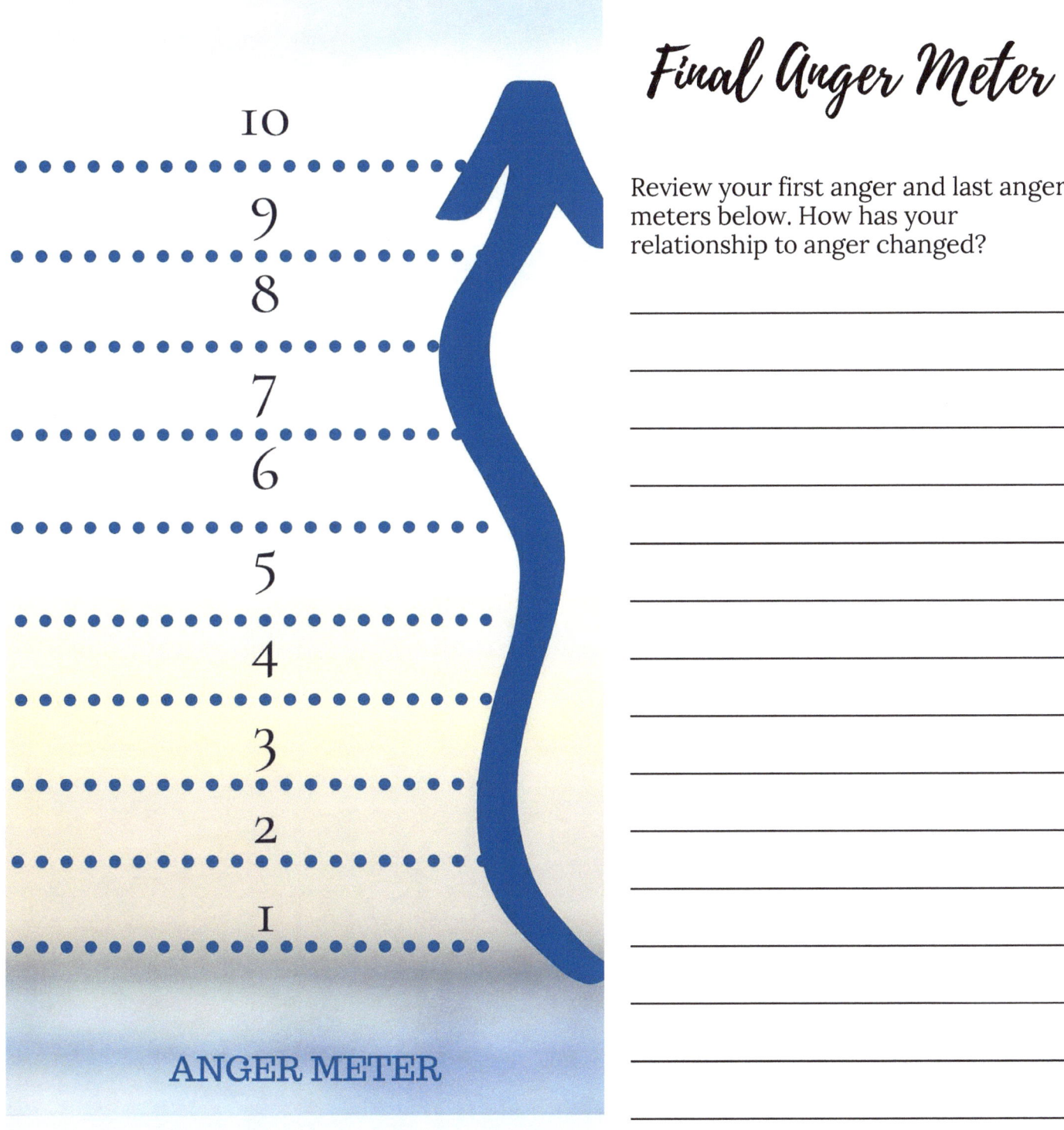

ANGER METER

For each day of the week, monitor and record the highest number you reach on the anger meter.

Monday

Turesday

Wedensday

Thursday

Friday

Saturday

Sunday

Check in Procedure
continued

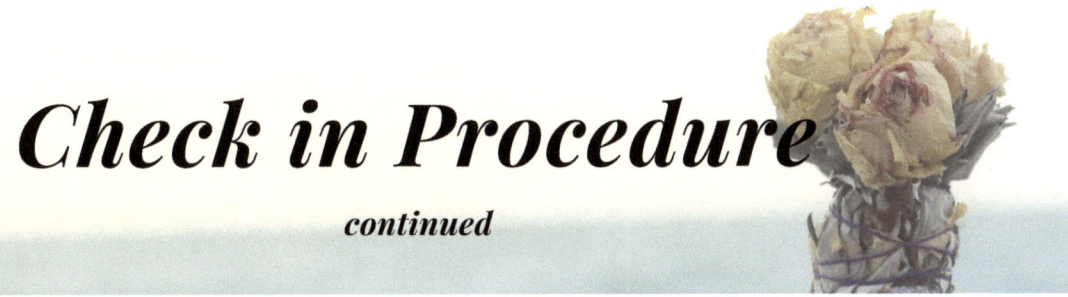

What where your physical cues:

What where your behavioral cues:

What where your cognitive cues:

Events, Cues and Strategies, identified during the check in procedure.

Ask yourself the following questions. Use the space below to see the progression as well as strategies in preventing acting out negatively in anger.

Question 1: What are my cues when I am becoming angry?

Question 2: What events appear to be triggers for me?

Question 3: What are some of strategies that are helpful in avoiding reaching an anger level that causes me to act out negatively?

Final Thoughts

Although from time to time I still struggle with anger, I have come to feel a disconnect within myself when I allow outside stressors to control my inner world.

The peace that I now feel inside is so valuable to me, when I trade it for anger or rage the disconnect feels as vast as the OCEAN. I feel a distinct disconnect. I feel the separation that it creates within myself and the gift of peace I have been given.

These tools greatly helped me in navigating my relationship with anger. The concepts with in this workbook continue to help me grow and remind me that I have a choice.

I wanted to create a course/program for other Christians who struggle with anger and shame themselves rather than learning why they turn to anger. As well as offer tools that can be used in this process. Applying the tools and techniques within this book can help change the relationship with anger.

God created us as emotional beings and it is up to us to seek Him and learn to navigate our emotions in a healthy way.

Thank you for taking them time to grow and learn. We are not meant to carry these burdens alone. God also created us for community and it is in community were we can find healing.

You are deeply loved, you are valued, you are seen and you are not alone.

Group Facilitator Guide
LEARNING TO MANAGE ANGER EFFECTIVELY

The Purpose of this material:

- Help individuals learn to manage anger effectively
- Stop violence or the threat of violence
- Develop self-control over thoughts and actions
- Receive support from others

If material is used for an Anger Management Program here are the Group Rules:

- **Safety:** No violence or threats of violence toward staff or other group members are permitted. It is very important that you view the group as a safe place to share your experiences and feelings without threats or fear of physical harm.

- **Confidentiality:** Group members should not discuss outside of the group what other participants say. What is shared in the group stays in the group.

- **Cross-talking:** Some group members find it difficult to share openly in a group setting. Being vulnerable can be scary. It is IMPORTANT to let people share without talking over them.

- **Homework Assignments:** Brief homework assignments will be given each week. Doing the homework assignments will improve your anger management skills and will allow you to get the most from the group experience.

- **Absences and Cancellations:** You should call or notify the Group Facilitator in advance if you cannot attend a group session. Because of the amount of material presented in each session, please do not miss more than three sessions.

    **If you miss more than three sessions, you may continue attending the weekly sessions, but you will not receive a certificate of completion. Unless you are meeting with a counselor/coach, they will discuss attendance expectations with you.

Group Facilitator Guide

LEARNING TO MANAGE ANGER EFFECTIVELY

Depending on the size of the group, each participant should have ample time to share. Limit sharing to the material that is covered and situations that arise regarding anger.

- Open the group up with a moment of prayer. Facilitator may ask if anyone wishes to open group.

- Ask participants to discuss any questions they may have regarding the previous weeks material.

- Ask participants to share their experience with anger over the previous week.

- After everyone has shared, begin to go over the Chapter material and ask participants to share along the way.

- Remind participants that this material is learned by review and participating in group is important.

- After group has completed the weekly chapter material, ask if anyone has any questions. Then review the Anger Meter and Check-in Queues and Question's.

- End the session by closing in prayer.

When all sessions are over, prepare "Completion Certificates" for the group participants that have successfully completed The Ocean That Separates Us - Anger Management Tools - Anger Management Class/Workshop.

CERTIFICATE of ACHIEVEMENT

THIS ACKNOWLEDGES THAT

AWESOME JOB. THIS CERTIFICATE IS AN EXAMPLE ONLY

HAS SUCCESSFULLY COMPLETED THE

The Ocean That Separates Us – Anger Management

FACILATOR IS TO SIGN

Facilitator Name, Organization, and Title

RHYTHMS OF THE SOUL
JENNI JACKSON CCLC, CPEF

www.ingramcontent.com/pod-product-compliance
Lightning Source LLC
Chambersburg PA
CBHW041548220426
43665CB00003B/62